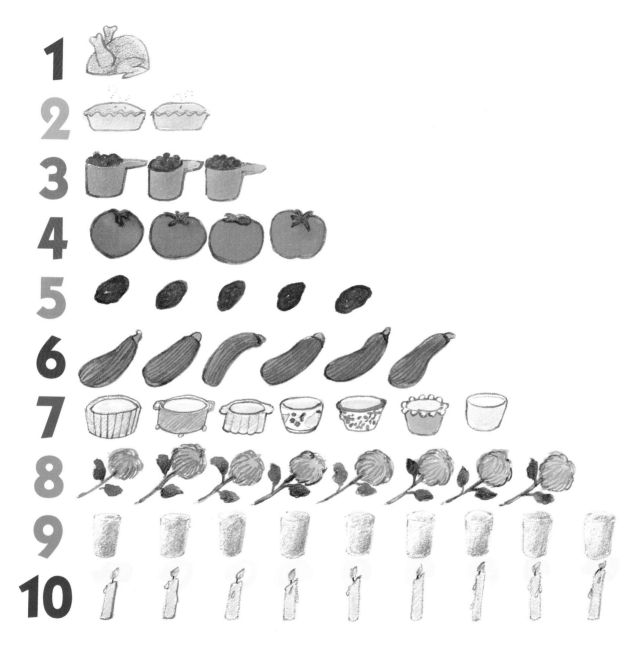

1, 2, 3 Thanksgiving!

To my daughters, Ylla and Larissa. W.N-L.
To Helen and Ronnie. Thanks for giving. R.K.

Text copyright © 1991 by W. Nikola-Lisa.

Illustrations copyright © 1991 by Robin Kramer.

Published in 1991 by Albert Whitman & Company,

6340 Oakton Street, Morton Grove, Illinois 60053.

Published simultaneously in Canada byGeneral Publishing, Limited, Toronto.

Printed in the United States of America.

10 9 8 7 6

Library of Congress Cataloging-in-Publication Data

Nikola-Lisa, W.

1,2,3 Thanksgiving! / W. Nikola-Lisa;

pictures by Robin Kramer.

p.   cm.

Summary: A Thanksgiving counting book depicting the numbers one through ten
through scenes of the holiday.

ISBN 0-8075-6109-6 (hardcover)

ISBN 0-8075-6110-X (paperback)

1. Counting—Juvenile literature. 2. Thanksgiving Day—Juvenile literature. [1. Thanksiving
Day. 2. Counting.] I. Kramer, Robin, ill.

II. Title. III. Title: One, two, three Thanksgiving!

QA113.N55   1991   90-28638

513.5'5—dc20   CIP

[E]   AC

The typeface for this book is Kabel Medium.

The illustration media are watercolor and colored pencil.

Cover and typography design: Karen Johnson Campbell.

W. Nikola-Lisa   illustrated by ROBIN KRAMER

1, 2, 3 Thanksgiving!

ALBERT WHITMAN & COMPANY
Morton Grove, Illinois

On Thanksgiving Day,
Papa stuffs one fat turkey,

Mama bakes two pumpkin pies,

Little Sister measures three cups of cranberries,

Uncle Martin washes four ripe tomatoes,

Baby Brother squishes five juicy raisins,

Big Sister slices six skinny squash,

Grandpa finds seven serving bowls,

Aunt Evelyn carries eight fresh flowers,

9

Cousin Raymond fills nine sparkling glasses,

and Grandma lights ten bright candles

as everyone pauses for a moment of silence

until Grandpa sings, "Let's eat!"

After dinner, Papa stacks ten empty plates,

Mama shakes nine crumpled napkins,

Little Sister clears eight round rolls,

Uncle Martin balances seven sturdy cups,

Baby Brother scatters six shiny spoons,

Big Sister catches five sugar cookies,

Grandpa snaps four quick pictures,

Aunt Evelyn plays three lively songs,

Cousin Raymond waves two wishbone halves,

and Grandma breaks into one big smile

as everyone gathers to give thanks
on this best-of-all Thanksgiving Day.

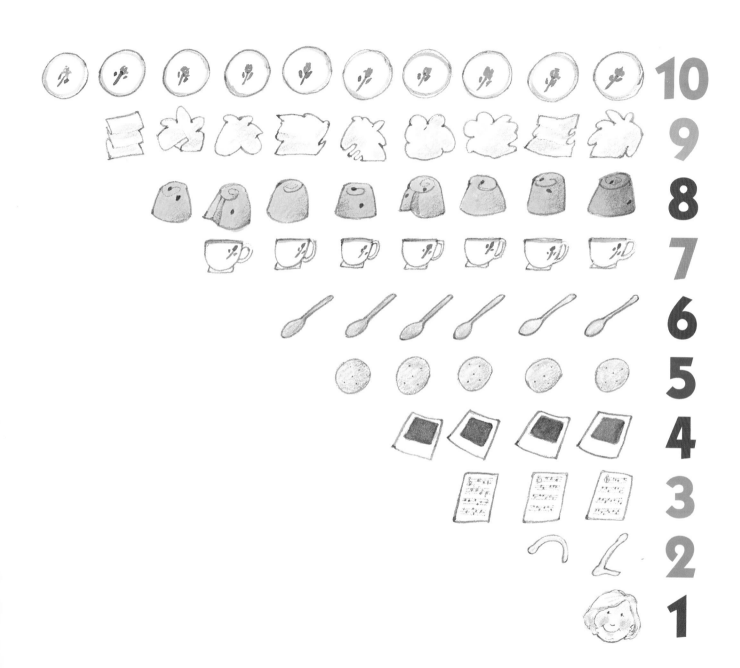